FOOD AND WINE PAIRING IN THREE STEPS

A GUIDE FOR THE HOSPITALITY AND BEVERAGE-RETAIL INDUSTRIES

JORDAN SHULER

Food And Wine Pairing In Three Steps

Editor: Rona Fleising

tellwell

Tellwell Talent
www.tellwell.ca

ISBN
978-1-77302-660-2 (Paperback)
978-1-77302-659-6 (eBook)

Contents

Foreword

I met Jordan when I was twenty-something, snowboarding in the Canadian Rocky Mountains and furiously pursuing an exciting career path to become a sommelier. At the time there was some chatter that my class was a lucky group, for we would be trained by a soft-spoken, Zen-like instructor named Jordan Shuler.

It became obvious early on Jordan was the personification of the proverb "still waters run deep" —he is one of the most engaging, introspective, and committed instructors I have known. Jordan fostered an interest level in you as a student, no matter where you came from, your background, or knowledge. You fundamentally enjoyed and trusted what he taught, and he constantly brought real-world applications to the classroom.

The fact Jordan begins this book by defining hospitality sets the tone for the 21st century sommelier. Jordan's voice is clear, as if the book is being spoken by him. His forest-through-the- trees approach of taking the whole concept and breaking it down into manageable pieces of information is what makes this text the most up-to-date and pleasurable read on the subject of food and wine pairing that I know of. It takes experience, reflection, and deep-rooted knowledge to speak about something so simply but in such a concise and accurate manner.

Food and Wine Pairing in Three Steps, A Guide for the Hospitality and Beverage-Retail Industries speaks to both the food and wine enthusiast, the student, as well as the seasoned professional. Fifty years from now the information printed here will be just as valid as it is today.

William Predhomme
Ontario's Best Sommelier (2011)
ASI Le Concours du Meilleur Sommelier du Monde (2013)
Ontario Hostelry Institute Fellow (2016)

January 2017
Toronto, Canada

Introduction

This guide functions as a complementary resource to your general wine studies. With the specific knowledge and tools presented here, you will learn how to think critically about the ingredients and flavors of food and how they interact with the ingredients and flavors of wine. These analytical skills, enriched by your growing knowledge of grape varieties and wine styles, will enable you to make skillful food and wine pairings.

Are You Hospitable?

Dr. Michael Dewer, Latin language specialist at the University of Toronto, explains the origin of hospitality: "The word 'hospitality' ultimately goes back to Latin 'hospes', a word used of someone with whom you have a friendship so close that you can expect to be welcome in each other's homes. This relationship was especially useful when you were traveling, as the homes of private individuals would likely be more comfortable in all kinds of ways than public inns, which were, it was thought, often dirty and even dangerous.

"There was, though, a later stage in the Middle Ages, when Christian charitable foundations would provide sleeping accommodation and food for pilgrims, travelers on their way to visit holy sites who were not usually personally known to them but whom they would regard as their 'brothers in Christ'. They might have also provided medical care, as travel in the Middle Ages could be very hard on the body and pilgrims might also be attacked by bandits intent on robbing them of any property they were carrying. The places where they offered such a welcome were 'hospices' or 'hospitals', places for offering the services of 'hospites' (the plural form of the original word 'hospes'). 'Hospitalitas' in medieval Latin is an abstract noun meaning 'the art or practice of being a hospes', and it passes into English as 'hospitality'" (personal communication, October 7, 2016).

In other words, those who ran hospices believed in taking care of pilgrims as well as they would take care of their own family and friends. What an admirable intention to carry into present day hospitality! Consider what the difference is between a stranger and a friend. Could the answer be as simple as time? Think of all the strangers we meet in our life who, after getting to know them, become friends. Our current friend is the same person who previously was a stranger, only time changes the way we see them; thus, we might as well treat them as a friend from the beginning.

When family and friends visit our home, we typically want them to feel comfortable and entertained; we might take them for a walk to point out some of the neighborhood highlights.

Selling and serving wine is actually quite similar. Customers want to feel comfortable and entertained, perhaps learn a thing or two. Each bottle of wine has a story behind it: Who made it? Where did it come from? What is the history and geography of that place? For many customers choosing a bottle of wine is not just shopping or quenching thirst; it's exploration.

A liquor store employee may think they're just selling wine, beer, and spirits to a thirsty public. While this is partly true, there are many customers who are looking for a bottle to help complete a meal, or shall we say complement a meal. When working retail the first question I ask my customers is whether the wine is going to be enjoyed with food or on its own. If they answer "with food" then I ask them to elaborate, and they're always happy to have found someone who will guide them to an appropriate choice. Many people enjoy cooking and especially cooking for others; serving a bottle of wine that will complement what they've prepared is part of the experience.

The few moments we have with our customers are an opportunity to take them on a cultural tour of our beverage menu or shop. Begin the tour with some interesting facts or stories about the wines and their appellations, then finish with a couple of recommendations and they are delighted!

Let us, in hospitality and beverage-retail settings, take care of our customers as hospitably as we would take care of our family and friends. Let us treat every customer as a guest.

The Principles of Food and Wine Pairing

IN THREE STEPS

Our guests typically know what they're going to eat before they know what they're going to drink. In restaurants, people look at the food options first. In retail, guests have an idea of what they're having for dinner and want a bottle to pair with it. Sometimes caterers are shopping for wine to pair with menus they've created for events. In all these scenarios, it is helpful and quite acceptable to discuss what they'll be eating. With just a few skillfully crafted questions we can gain enough information to make some pairing suggestions. Keep in mind, we must remain flexible in our approach. Our customers might be telling us they enjoy a particular wine and we're thinking that it's not a good match for the dish they're about to eat; in this scenario, we should only share our opinion if requested. Our guests' satisfaction is paramount; if they have a personal preference then that's what we should sell them, regardless of whether we think it's a suitable match or not.

Now let's get to it. What follows is a three-step process to help us make excellent food and wine pairings.

Step One

MATCH THE ELEMENTS OF THE DISH WITH THE ELEMENTS OF THE WINE

In this context, elements refer to the five tastes (bitter, salty, sour, sweet, umami) as well as any other possible ingredients or factors that influence how we taste food. Consider all the elements on the plate, not just the main ingredient.

BITTER

Bitter foods, except coffee, do not enter our diet as commonly as those that are salty, sweet, or sour. If you do come across a dish with bitter elements, like arugula, olives, or rapini, then avoid wines high in tannin which would compound the bitter taste. Instead, look for wines with some sweetness which coats the palate and lessens the bitterness.

MATCH

Bitter food with off-dry wine

AVOID

Bitter food with tannic (high-tannin) wine

SALTY

Salt can function as a tenderizer on meat or as added acidity in a dish that tastes flat. A little salt on food has no enemies in wine, though be careful as our perception of salt will increase with the presence of tannin and alcohol. Both acid and sugar stimulate the organs in our palate (salivary glands) to produce saliva. This moisture serves well to dilute an overly salty dish.

MATCH

Salty food with acidic (generous acid) or sweet wine

AVOID

Salty food with high alcohol wine
Salty food with tannic wine

SOUR

Our perception of sourness is affected by the amounts and types of acid in our food and drink. Acid is a common ingredient in our diet, though most people rarely think about it. If we can remember eating food that tasted sour or drinking a beverage that felt sharp, then we've experienced the effects of acidity. Acid functions to give food and drink volume, or as I say in the classroom, acid gives food life—spreading and lifting flavors around our mouth and up to the roof of our palate. Consider how low-acid food and drink feel flat on our tongue. A low-acid wine would be overwhelmed by high-acid food; a high-acid wine would taste sour with low-acid food. When pairing food and wine, acidity levels should be equal.

Pairing semi-sweet wines with high-acid foods also works well; sugar and acid are quite friendly as is evidenced in some cuisines that traditionally combine the tastes of sweet and sour.

As previously mentioned, acidity functions to stimulate our salivary glands to produce saliva. This moisture can be soothing when our palate is full of salt or, as will be explained, helps comfort a palate full of heat (from spice).

Match

Acidic food with acidic or off-dry wine
Medium-acid food with medium-acid wine
Low-acid food with low-acid wine

SWEET

Most people can confidently describe what they're eating or drinking as dry or sweet. In beverages, sugar and other sweet ingredients create a creamy mouthfeel and contribute to a drink's overall weight. When it comes to pairings think sweet with sweet. A rich dessert coats the palate with flavor. Choose a wine that does the same, so that both are tasted and neither is overwhelmed by the other.

Though not as efficient as acid, sugar also functions to stimulate saliva production in most palates and can be helpful when pairing with salty food or heat.

MATCH

Dry food with dry wine
Medium-sweet food with medium-sweet wine
Sweet food with wine that is at least as sweet as the food

UMAMI

Umami is the relative newcomer to the family of tastes (bitter, salty, sour, sweet, umami). This Japanese discovery translates to English as savory and can more casually be used to refer to a dish being rich and flavorful. Foods high in umami tend to have generous amounts of glutamic acid: aged cheeses, shellfish, cured meats, soy sauce, and ripe tomatoes. Adding these ingredients to a plate of food will often, positively, increase the intensity of flavor. We are still exploring how to cook and make pairings with this fifth taste. Common sense tells us a rich and flavorful dish would pair with a rich and flavorful wine; in other words, an umami dish deserves an umami wine.

MATCH

Umami food with umami wine (aged wines or wines made from overly-ripe fruit)

PROTEIN

Of all the various forms of protein we find in our food, it is specifically the animal-sourced protein that pairs well with the tannin in wine. Most wine drinkers know the word tannin without any knowledge of its source, nature, or function. Tannins are found in red grape skins. Any wine that has natural color, from skin contact during fermentation, will also have some level of tannic content. Tannins belong to a complex group of organic compounds called polyphenols of which we find various types in the world all around us: wood; black tea leaves; dark chocolate; almond skins; grape seeds, skins, and stalks.

In wine, tannins act as antioxidants and preservatives, helping wines age and remain healthy. In our palate, tannins from food and drink inhibit our salivary glands' ability to produce saliva and as a result, our palates dry out—sometimes described as a feeling of our mouth puckering up.

There are valid reasons to explain why the wine world does not speak much about tannins, other than their drying effect on the palate. I asked Dr. Ron Jackson of Brock University to explain exactly the nature and function of tannins. He responded with a creative analogy: "Tannins are one of the most complex group of organic compounds found in nature. They are all based on one of two major groups of phenolics: flavonoid and non-flavonoids. They come in many distinct forms that can change character based on a wine's pH level, presence of oxygen and sulfur dioxide, and innumerable other conditions. They can polymerize with themselves and other constituents found in wine and food, and are sequentially modified (usually broken down into simpler constituents or totally decomposed) as they move through the digestive tract. For the researcher, it is the equivalent of trying to track the movement and action of animals through a thick forest where the animals can change shape and form as they move" (personal communication, October 1, 2016).

Does science know of a relationship between tannins and digestion? Dr. Jackson says, "There are no simple answers...we know they have an effect on digestive enzymes though that effect is not yet clear" (Rohn *et al.*, 2002; Gu *et al.*, 2011).

Some people have an aversion to red wine thinking it's too bitter. I believe they must have, at one time, drunk tannic red wine without food and experienced the puckering feeling of a dried palate; a better experience would have been to drink low-tannin red wine without food. Tannin pairs well with animal proteins which reduce our perception of bitterness—the more protein in a dish, the more tannin it can handle in a wine. Denser, fattier pieces of protein would call for a more tannic wine, and lighter proteins would only need a small amount.

It is common knowledge among sommeliers that tannic wines react negatively when paired with certain foods, causing a metallic flavor in the palate. Research from Japan explains that it is the iron found in most tannic wines that reacts with fatty acids like those found in salmon, walnuts, oysters, and spinach (*Science Illustrated*, 2010). Be cautious and stay away from tannin when pairing with these foods.

MATCH

Animal protein with the tannin in wine

AVOID

Foods rich in fatty acids with tannic wine

HEAT

In this context, heat refers to certain warming spices such as West Indian jerk, East Indian curry, Mexican chili, Thai galanga, Japanese ginger and wasabi. When pairing with foods that have heat avoid high alcohol wine—ethanol's volatility spreads that spice throughout the palate and beyond, creating some discomfort. Avoid tannin as well—a dry mouth from a tannic wine is not a welcome environment for spice. Instead, an appropriate pairing for heat is acid and/or sugar; both will comfort the palate by promoting saliva production, thus reducing the perception of heat in the palate.

MATCH

Heat with wines containing generous acid and/or sugar

AVOID

Heat with high-alcohol wine
Heat with tannic wine

WEIGHT

Weight in food comes primarily from fat, protein, and sugar. A wine's weight, called body, comes from alcohol, tannin, and sugar. A wine described as light-bodied means it feels light and thin on the palate. A fitting analogy is to think about milk and how it sits on the palate: skim milk is light-bodied; 2% milk is medium-bodied; 10% cream is full-bodied. A light-bodied wine would be completely overwhelmed by a heavy dish, with most if not all of the subtle flavors in the wine being masked by the heavier food; we might as well drink water. Likewise, a full-bodied wine would just be too much for a light dish.

MATCH

A light (weight) dish with light-bodied wine
A medium dish with medium-bodied wine
A heavy dish with full-bodied wine

INTENSITY OF FLAVOR

Intensity of flavor is related to weight and body, whereby intensely-flavored food is often also heavy on the palate and intensely-flavored wines are often full-bodied. Because there are some wonderful exceptions to this trend it is wise to consider these two elements (weight and intensity of flavor) separately. Anyone who enjoys sprinkling shaved truffles onto their pasta or drizzling truffle oil into a soup knows how much intensity this light-weight mushroom contributes to a dish's overall flavor.

Marlborough Sauvignon Blanc is an example of a light bodied white wine with high intensity of flavor. Cool-climate Cabernet Sauvignon, especially from a wet vintage, is an example of a full-bodied red wine with low intensity of flavor.

Adding a sauce to a dish impacts many of the elements already discussed and needs to be included when thinking about a pairing. Consider how intensity of flavor changes if a chicken breast is dressed in white wine sauce versus pesto versus creamy mustard.

Food preparation methods will also affect flavor intensity. A boiled potato does not taste like a fried one, nor does a baked fish have much resemblance to one that has been grilled.

MATCH

Flavor intensity (food) with flavor intensity (wine)

TEXTURE

Texture, sometimes referred to as mouthfeel, should also be considered when making a pairing, yet we have room for flexibility. Sometimes a dish can be paired with two wines that have different textures; for example, creamy soup pairs well with either a creamy wine or a sharp, acidic wine. We can gauge what style our guest prefers. (Someone with acid reflux might prefer the creamy wine, while another who enjoys light-bodied wines might choose the more acidic one.)

Rich, fatty foods pair well with acidic wines as acid helps clean fat from our palate. If fat is combined with protein, then tannin is the ideal accompaniment.

MATCH

Creamy food with acidic or sweet wine
Fatty food with acidic wine
Fatty protein with tannic wine

Step Two

COMPLEMENT THE FLAVORS OF THE DISH WITH THE FLAVORS OF THE WINE

Match the flavors in the food to similar flavors in the wine. That said, it is interesting to note there are sommeliers who enjoy looking for wines that have contrasting flavor profiles to the dish they're pairing. A classic example of a pairing that succeeds despite its contrasting flavors is foie gras with Sauternes: the pâté of foie gras has an earthy, meaty flavor profile that is delicious when paired with the honeyed, tropical flavors of Sauternes—a nobly-rotted, white, dessert wine. Normally, an earthy, meaty dish would pair with an earthy, meaty wine—not one with honey and tropical fruit flavors—though it works in this unique instance and works beautifully. The foie gras with Sauternes is a pairing based on matching fat with acid, weight with body, intensity with intensity, and umami with umami. There are not many wines with as much intensity and umami as Sauternes. This type of exceptional pairing, with contrasting flavors, is difficult to create on the spot, especially in a hospitality or retail setting; thus, a more reliable technique is to consider the aromas and flavors of a dish and complement those with similar aromas and flavors in a wine. To begin, think in broad flavor categories like earthy, floral, fruity, herbal, spicy, vegetal, or even obscure flavor categories reminiscent of animals or minerals. If a dish has flavors belonging to one or more of these categories, then so too should our wine choice.

Dear friends and I recently shared a bottle of truffle-flavored wine they had purchased at a shop in the Luberon region of Provence, France. We were all quite excited to taste this precious nectar, yet on first sip everyone was trying to hide their disgust. Perhaps flavoring wine with fungus was not a good idea. We left the bottle on the counter and started preparing a light, festive dinner: arugula salad, olives, and aged cheddar, followed by fried onion and potato pancakes. A few bites into dinner we remembered our still half-filled wine glasses were sitting on the counter, so we brought them to the table and cautiously took another sip. The wine was delicious with the food! We were eating a dinner consisting of only earthy-flavored ingredients and only an earthy-flavored wine would have been a pleasing complement.

François Chartier, a Quebec-based sommelier, is researching food and wine pairing at a molecular level. His work has helped identify the molecules responsible for flavor. François describes large aromatic families and suggests pairing food and wine that have aromas belonging to the same family. In his book, *Taste Buds and Molecules,* he shares the experience of looking for a wine to match with a traditional Middle Eastern salad called tabbouleh. The salad includes tomatoes, chopped parsley, mint, bulgur, salt, oil, and lemon juice. According to the principles we are learning in this guide, the salad would require a crisp (high acid), dry, light-bodied wine without tannin and an earthy, herbal, citrus flavor profile. There are many wines in the world that fit these requirements, so which would be the best choice? François would suggest the answer lies in a molecular understanding of the two dominant flavors in the salad—mint and parsley. These two ingredients belong to what François calls the anise-flavored family, and so he would say the perfect pairing would also have flavors belonging to this family; it turns out there are quite a few:

Whites
Albariño, Chardonnay, Chenin Blanc, Greco di Tufo, Riesling, and Sauvignon Blanc

Reds
Syrah (Shiraz), Cabernet/Shiraz blends, and Grenache-based blends

Two of these wines fill all our aforementioned requirements of being crisp, dry, and light-bodied without any tannin: Chenin Blanc and Sauvignon Blanc. A cool climate (generous acidity) Grenache would also fit these requirements, especially if it has gone through a winemaking technique called carbonic maceration, which creates a red wine with minimal tannin.

As we gain experience with wine tasting, our nose and palate become sensitive to aromas and flavors, and our ability to categorize them improves. Eventually, we are able to describe aromas and flavors not only using broad categories but with very specific terminology. With practice and confidence, a dish once described as “spicy” might become a dish with “crushed black pepper”; a “fruity-flavored” dessert might become an “apricot-flavored” dessert. In this latter example, a decent wine pairing would have a generally fruity flavor profile, but an excellent wine pairing would have an apricot flavor profile.

Step Three

ASK YOUR GUESTS IF THEY HAVE A PREFERENCE FOR COLOR OF WINE

After we've gathered all the information we need from Steps One and Two, we let our guests tell us what color wine they would like. This is genuine hospitality.

There used to be a wine-pairing expression: *white wine with fish, red wine with meat.* This expression made life easy for a hospitality or beverage professional. In fact, one did not need to be a professional at all in order to follow the principle of this expression. The problem was, guests would often receive a wine pairing suggestion they did not enjoy.

Remember, the underlying rule of food and wine pairing is to be flexible. If our guests are having fish and want a red wine, who are we to say no! Sure, they can have a red wine; we now know it is important to direct them to one of our lower tannin options because we do not want to create metallic flavors from pairing tannin with fatty acids. If known, we could recommend a wine that was fermented in stainless steel, not oak barrels—even less tannin. Examples include most New Zealand Pinot Noirs; French and Canadian Gamays; young Spanish Garnachas; and Italian Valpolicellas.

See Appendix 2 for more details on oak barrels and their effect on wine

If steak is on the menu, we now know the importance of finding a tannic wine for the animal protein. The world is full of tannic red wines and some tannic pink wines, but what about white wines? A skilled hospitality or beverage professional understands that an oak-fermented or oak-aged white wine contains tannin and could pair quite nicely with that piece of meat. Examples include aged white Rioja; Hunter Valley Semillon; some Côte de Beaune Blanc; and some California Chardonnays.

With so many styles of varietal and blended wines from around the world we should be able to fill most, if not all, of our requirements from Steps One and Two with either a white, pink, or red wine—whatever our guests prefer.

When All Else Fails

Some classical dishes are quite complex, with ingredients and flavors that challenge even the most skilled professional to make a first-rate wine pairing; an example is Spaghetti Bolognese.

A typical recipe for this dish has the following ingredients:

INGREDIENTS FOR SPAGHETTI BOLOGNESE

Fresh tomatoes **Tomato sauce**	lots of acid requires an acidic wine
Sugar	usually a couple teaspoons and also sugar from the tomatoes; requires an off-dry wine
Ground beef or **bacon**	protein requires tannin
Salt or **stock**	requires a wine with some acidity and/or sugar, without too much tannin
Pasta	contributes quite a bit of weight to the dish; requires a medium to full-bodied wine
Onions and **garlic**	contribute heat and intensity of flavor; require acid and/or sugar and intensity of flavor
Parmesan	contributes saltiness and flavor; requires acid though can handle some tannin (see Appendix 1)
Olive oil	contributes texture and flavor; requires a wine with generous acidity and earthy flavors
Herbs, often oregano and thyme	contribute flavor; require a wine with herbal flavors

We're left wondering whether our wine choice needs lots of tannin for the protein or not too much because of the salt. There are also many flavors in the dish: earthy, herbal, and meaty. Which one should we match to the wine?

In these unique situations, if our analysis of the ingredients and flavors does not help us come to a clear wine selection, then we should investigate the cultural origin of the dish. Often the country or region that first created a dish also created a wine style, or another beverage, to drink with it.

With the example of Spaghetti Bolognese the origin is North-Central Italy, the city of Bologna. What do the locals drink in Bologna? There is a white wine called Malvasia which, when fermented in a barrel into an off-dry style, contains enough acidity and intensity of flavor to make an appropriate pairing with our spaghetti.

The local red wine is Sangiovese, a medium-to full-bodied wine with generous acidity, some sugar, medium tannin, and an earthy, herbal, sometimes meaty, flavor profile. It's the ideal wine for our spaghetti as both the wine and the dish are complex in similar ways.

Final Thoughts

Like all new endeavours, this three-step process of food and wine pairing requires practice.

At first it may seem like a lot to think about, but there is no need to rush. We should feel comfortable to think out loud; in fact, most customers appreciate listening to and thus learning from our rationale.

Although this guide is focussed on pairing food to wine, it would be wise to remember that other beverages can also complement a dish. A well-designed beverage menu or skillfully-stocked liquor store will offer a variety of beverage options: a wide range of ales and lagers; a few styles of sake; various liqueurs and spirits (the ingredients of cocktails). Sometimes a situation calls for a non-alcoholic beverage pairing, and we can be creative with these too: sparkling water flavored with elderflower syrup; jasmine green tea with a drop of grapefruit bitters; mochaccino with a sprinkle of cinnamon; ginger beer with half a teaspoon of maple syrup. Wine is perhaps the friendliest food-pairing beverage, though keep all the others in mind.

Lastly, I would like to encourage you to use this knowledge to help advance our professions. By improving service excellence our guests will enjoy their experience and we will feel better about our work. Act hospitably and treat every customer as your guest.

With Gratitude

Richard Harvey

Richard is highly intelligent and humble—two qualities rarely seen in the same individual. I trained to become a sommelier under Richard, both studying in the classroom and working at his wine boutique; it was the best training I've ever received. Today, as a college beverage professor, I try to emulate for my students the way Richard's wine stories spurred my passion.

Gail Norton

Gail is a chef extraordinaire and savvy entrepreneur. I was inspired by her ability to create and manage a variety of enterprises: boutique grocery; catering company; culinary magazine; cooking schools; restaurants in Canada and France. Gail showed me how to cook. To this day, whenever I smell someone sweating onions or roasting duck I think back to our exploits in the kitchen.

Janet Webb

Janet is a pioneer of Alberta's privatized wine-retail industry and is responsible for launching many industry-professionals' careers. She gave me my first break into the industry, hiring me for her wine shop even though my beverage knowledge was limited. She encouraged and sponsored me to train as a sommelier—an especially kind gesture considering it laid the foundation for my career. My firm belief in service excellence stems from observing Janet at work.

Appendix 1

A WORD ON CHEESE

Cheese is often served as an assortment on a board or platter. Examples could include a selection of young and aged cheeses from buffalo, cow, goat, and sheep; some firm, others soft; with edible rinds or not; and possibly flavored with ingredients like herbs, garlic, or smoke.

A dilemma arises when considering a wine pairing for these assorted cheese boards: whether to choose a wine that will pair perfectly with one of the cheeses and might not pair so well with the others, or a wine that will pair just decently with all the cheeses.

For example since goat cheese is quite acidic, light weight, and earthy flavored, an ideal pairing would be an acidic, light-bodied, earthy-flavored wine. If that same wine is paired with a board of various cheeses it might be fine for one or two but would probably be overwhelmed by any heavier, more intensely-flavored cheeses and would not complement any cheese flavors other than earth.

SPECIFIC CONSIDERATIONS:

- Young cheese contains more water and is thus creamier than aged cheese.
- Cheese aromas and flavors become more pronounced with age.
- Unpasteurized cheeses are more flavorful than pasteurized.
- Blue cheeses are salty and intensely flavored; balance salt with sugar and choose a sweet, intensely flavored wine.
- Goat milk cheeses are high in acid and tend to have earthy, mineral, and citrus flavor profiles.
- Sheep milk cheeses tend to be smooth with nutty flavor profiles.
- Cheese is unique to other food and wine pairings in that salt and tannin can pair well together when the cheese is strongly-flavored and firm, like Parmigiano-Reggiano.

Appendix 2

A WORD ON WOOD

If wine is fermented in a wooden barrel then that material, most often oak, will have an influence on the final product: color will advance; tannic levels will increase; aroma and flavor profiles will adopt wood-based characteristics. Most barrel interiors are fire-toasted to some degree and this process contributes various aromas, flavors, and tannin to a wine that is either aging or fermenting inside the barrel. A generously-toasted barrel will contribute smokiness to a wine. These oak-fermented wines can pair nicely with smoked foods (ribs, salmon, tofu, etc.). American Oak contains vanillin and some European Oaks have spice. These aromas and flavors can often be perceived in wines that have spent time in the barrel.

Appendix 3

A WORD ON ROSÉ

There is an assortment of pink wine styles around the world; some are created from blending white and red wines together, though the majority are made from red grapes alone. By reducing the amount of time that juice and skin are in contact during fermentation (maceration), these wines do not receive as much color or tannin as a red wine.

Pink wine, or rosé if one prefers to use its French name, is food friendly. With the exception of California White Zinfandel, which is a sweet wine from one grape variety, most rosés are dry or off-dry blends of two or more varieties. These wines can have a significant level of complexity, with flavors from each grape in the blend, often with similar acid levels to whites and less tannin than reds.

Here is a list of common rosés:

LIGHT-BODIED

GRAPE (APPELLATION)	TYPICAL TASTE	FLAVOR PROFILE
Baga (Portugal)	dry, acidic	citrus, herbs and smoke
Pinot Noir (Canada)	dry to off-dry, acidic	raspberry, floral and earth

MEDIUM-BODIED

GRAPE (APPELLATION)	TYPICAL TASTE	FLAVOR PROFILE
Cabernet Franc (Loire Valley, France)	dry, medium acidity	red berries and floral
Sangiovese (Italy)	dry, acidic	floral and melons
White Zinfandel (California, U.S.A.)	sweet, medium acidity	red fruit, floral and melons
Tempranillo-based blends (Spain)	dry, medium acidity	herbs and meat

FULL-BODIED

GRAPE (APPELLATION)	TYPICAL TASTE	FLAVOR PROFILE
Mourvèdre-based blends (Provence, France)	dry, medium acidity	cherries and rose petals
Grenache/Cinsault blends (Tavel, France)	dry, medium acidity	strawberry and spice

Appendix 4

PRACTICE ASSIGNMENT

Find A Wine Pairing For This Dish

Rack of Lamb with Tomatoes and Mustard Greens, Lemon-based Dressing

Step One

MATCH THE ELEMENTS OF THE DISH WITH THE ELEMENTS OF WINE

DISH	REQUIRES A WINE WITH
BITTER yes/no	
SALTY low/medium/high	
SOUR low/medium/high	
SWEET dry/off-dry/medium/sweet	
UMAMI yes/no	
PROTEIN yes/no	
HEAT yes/no	
WEIGHT light/medium/heavy	
FLAVOR low intensity/high intensity	
TEXTURE creamy/sharp/smooth/astringent	

Step Two

COMPLEMENT THE FLAVORS OF THE DISH WITH THE FLAVORS OF WINE

DOMINANT FLAVORS IN DISH	YES	NO
chemical		
earthy		
floral		
fruity		
herbal		
nutty		
spicy		
vegetal		
woody		
mineral		
meaty		
other		

NOW CONSIDER THE WORLD OF WINE TO FIND THREE APPROPRIATE PAIRINGS

INCLUDE GRAPE(S) AND APPELLATION (AGRICULTURAL ORIGIN)

USE THE LIST OF WINES IN APPENDIX 5 FOR SOME IDEAS

WHITE

PINK

RED

Appendix 5

GLOSSARY OF COMMON GRAPES AND WINES

Listed by Weight, Alphabetically

Grape or Style (Major Appellations)

WHITES

Light-Bodied

Alvarinho and Loureiro (Vinho Verde)
Assyrtiko (Greece)
Dry Riesling (Austria/Australia)
Fino Sherry (Jerez)
Garganega (Soave)
Muscat (Alsace/Piedmont)
Pinot Grigio (Italy)
Prosecco (Italian sparkling)
Sauvignon Blanc (Bordeaux/New Zealand/Loire Valley)
Verdejo (Rueda)

Medium-Bodied

Albariño (Rías Baixas)
Amontillado Sherry (Jerez)
Cava (Spanish sparkling)
Champagne (French sparkling)
Crémant (French sparkling)
Dry Chenin Blanc (Loire Valley/South Africa)
Gewurztraminer (Alsace)
Grüner Veltliner (Austria)
Off-dry Riesling (Canada/Germany)
Pinot Gris (Alsace/Oregon)
Sekt (German sparkling)
Unoaked Chardonnay (Chablis/Niagara)

Full-Bodied

Marsanne, Roussanne blends (Rhone Valley)
Oaked Chardonnay (Burgundy/Australia/California)
Oloroso Sherry (Jerez)
Semillon (Australia/Bordeaux)
Sweet Chenin Blanc (Loire Valley)
Viognier (Northern Rhone Valley/Australia)

REDS

Light-Bodied

Cinsault (Southern France)
Corvina-based blends (Valpolicella)
Dolcetto (Piedmont)
Gamay (Beaujolais/Niagara)
Pinot Noir (Burgundy/New Zealand/Oregon)

Medium-Bodied

Grenache (Côtes-du-Rhône/Sardinia)
Sangiovese (Central Italy)
Tempranillo (Spain)

Full-Bodied

Cabernet Sauvignon-based blends (Bordeaux/Bulgaria/California/Washington State)
Corvina-based blends from dehydrated grapes (Amarone della Valpolicella)
Grenache-based blends (Southern Rhone Valley/Spain)
Malbec (Argentina/South West France)
Merlot-based blends (Bordeaux/California/Chile)
Nebbiolo (Piedmont)
Petite Sirah (California)
Syrah (Australia/Northern Rhone Valley)
Zinfandel (California)

SWEET WINES

Light-Bodied

Moscato (Asti)

Medium-Bodied

Barrel-aged Port (Douro)
Ice Wine (Austria/Canada/Germany)
Late harvest wine (Canada/Germany)
Nobly-rotted wine (Austria/Bordeaux/Loire Valley/Tokaji)
Vin Doux Naturel (Southern France)

Full-Bodied

Banyuls and Maury (Southern France)
Bottle-aged Port (Douro)
Pedro Ximénez Sherry (Jerez)
Recioto (Valpolicella)

References

Chartier, François (2011). *Taste Buds and Molecules.* Toronto: McClelland & Stewart

Jackson, Ron S. (2000). *Wine Science: Principles, Practice, Perception.* San Diego: Academic Press (2010). *Science Illustrated,* (1). 18.

Wine Folly. (2013). *What Are Tannins in Wine?* Retrieved October 19, 2016, from http://winefolly.com/review/what-are-tannins-in-wine/

About the Author

Jordan Shuler is a professor and sommelier living in Toronto, Canada.

Jordan has a well-rounded knowledge and skill set attained through formal sommelier training and experience with luxury cruise ships and hotels, fine-dining restaurants, and specialty wine boutiques. He has cycled thousands of miles through the wine nations of the world and worked for winemakers in Alsace, France and Mosel, Germany. As a beverage professor at George Brown College he instructs students in the Culinary, Hospitality and Continuing Education Departments. In addition, Jordan recently joined the Liquor Control Board of Ontario (LCBO) returning to beverage-retail and the opportunity to serve the public hospitably.

Lightning Source UK Ltd.
Milton Keynes UK
UKOW05f0646270417
300019UK00011B/170/P

9 781773 02660